Italic Handwriting & Calligraphy
for the Beginner

Italic Handwriting
& Calligraphy
for the Beginner

A Craft Manual

Charles Lehman

 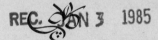
A Pentalic Book
Taplinger Publishing Company
NEW YORK

Published in 1982 by
TAPLINGER PUBLISHING CO., INC.
New York, New York

Library of Congress Catalog Card Number: 80-53415
ISBN 0-8008-4291-X

Design: Charles Lehman
Typography: Irish Setter

For Dolores, Anna, Chris and David

Table of Contents

Preface

THE BEGINNING Italic writer gets more than he bargained for, but in the best sense. In addition to being able to write a fluent, legible hand, his friends come to regard him as a kind of genius! Their observations may be embarrassing, but his admirers know what they are talking about, for almost from the beginning of his work with the Italic nib, the writer's efforts take on a graceful order. The thick-thin rhythm which characterizes the Italic hand makes ballpoint pen writing seem drab, and the remarkable thing is that the broadedged pen itself does the work of patterning the attractive strokes in the right places. Writing suddenly becomes a pleasure and this, more than anything, is the reason for the widespread interest in Italic.

In addition to its elegance the Italic hand is practical. Writing Italic is that rare activity that is both beautiful and useful. This, in fact, is the whole message of the modern revival of work in traditional modes; the crafts offer something worthwhile to one's everyday life, and given the frustration that most people have with their own handwriting, the reasonable Italic methods are a welcome change. Writers are well aware that a miserable scrawl passed from grocery list to bank checks guarantees frequent mistakes of interpretation, to say nothing of the permanent ugliness of its appearance. A change is clearly called for, and Italic is the answer for reviving the craft of handwriting.

Italic is fun to learn and results in fine work for two reasons. First, the letters feature simple, accident-free shapes that slope slightly to the right and hold up under the pressure of speed; elliptical curves are natural to the hand as it pushes and pulls in the rhythm of writing, and safe joining practices help to control the writing pattern.

Second, Italic is a tight, rhythmic hand with continuous sweeps of thicks and thins that make up a rich, colorful writing pattern. Italic, in short, applies the same principles to handwriting that appears in all fine crafts: *angles* for strength and *curves* for gracefulness. As one calligrapher wrote, handwriting is 'everyman's craft.' This is to say that the average person can enjoy making handwriting that is artistic. It sounds almost too simple, yet that is the secret of the craft of writing itself. Good handwriting serves as its own best ornament. The way to achieve it is with reliable tools, simple working techniques and the beautiful, flowing Italic models.

Introduction

THE OUTLINE of this book and the design of
individual practice pages follow a traditional
pattern for learning. To write Italic handwriting
and calligraphy well, the learner must, first of
all, understand the work that is to be done—in
brief, *get the idea* of what is to be accomplished
and how best to proceed; then *practice carefully*—
with attention to the quality of the work, with
the purpose of making beautiful writing kept in
view. Finally, the writing must be evaluated
frequently for possible improvement—*adjust the
results*. This is accomplished not only by correcting basic mistakes, but also by learning from the
work of expert scribes.

   To provide the learner with understanding of
the skills needed for Italic handwriting, PART
ONE examines characteristics resulting from
production of ordinary handwriting that make it
a craft in its own right with its own criteria of

quality. Chapter One defines the properties of handwriting as they appear in key historic models and provides a brief history of the origin of Italic letter design. Chapter Two presents a basic explanation of traditional materials needed to write Italic letters. In this way the study of letterform and movement in handwriting leads the beginning writer directly toward the practical preparation needed to begin writing. The use of paper, ink and the traditional edged pen is explained in relation to the basic ideas underlying modern Italic writing.

PART TWO features practice pages designed for learning letterforms and wordforms (joined letters) and simple ideas for page layout (pageforms). Chapter Three illustrates detailed designs of each letter including diagrams of stroke number, sequence and direction and illustration of how to use the letter in joined writing. Large and small scale sample letters are presented with illustrations that highlight critical features of letterform. Chapter Four provides comprehensive information about joining letters into words. A brief treatment of page layout follows in Chapter Five to help the beginning writer understand the function of margins and traditional procedures for arranging single and double page formats.

PART THREE brings together samples of formal and informal writings by various scribes. It also includes a select bibliography to acquaint the beginner with the possibilities for greater understanding of the craft of writing.

Part One

CHAPTER ONE

Cursive Handwriting in History

CURSIVE HANDWRITING, the day-to-day, ordinary handwriting used for informal purposes, has always existed alongside formal scribal models. It stood in relation to the formal work in much the same way that handwriting stands today in relation to typography. Yet, ordinary handwriting has always been considered a craft in its own right. Over the centuries it has developed its own criteria of quality that guide the learner to understand and then perform rhythmic writing through careful practice. As the personal expression of a writer, ordinary handwriting will range in appearance from disciplined and refined to casual and coarse, reflecting the temperament and effort of the writer. However, the most important considerations— qualities of handwriting that contribute to ease of reading—are found in the practicality and attractiveness of the letter designs used for the writing. Practical, beautiful writing results from sensible use of letter models that are appropriate both to the hand of the writer and to the eye of the reader. Elaborate, embellished letterforms that are time-consuming to perform and accident prone in rapid writing must be rejected in favor of more reasonable movements—handwriting models that suggest spirited, expressive

WE HAVE SEEN HIS STAR IN THE EAST
AND ARE COME TO WORSHIP HIM.ᴹᵃᵀ.

Modern Formal Writing based on an ancient model.

ʌᏏᴄᏒᴇ⨍Ᏻ🇭🇮ᴋ🇱ᴍᏰ

Early Roman Cursive, 3rd C. BC to 3rd C.

movements as an enrichment, an extension, of their forms but in a harmonized durable framework—rhythmic patterned structures that are both easy to make and comfortable to the eye of the reader.

Although a happy marriage of beauty and strength is rare in handwriting models, Italic designs dance in a lively way and always to the same tune. Simplified letters slope slightly to the right in picket-fence patterns with softly arching tops that crest out of branching strokes; spacing between letters is compressed, and forms join frequently in a durable, patterned flow that had

Primieramente imparerai di fare que=
sti dui tratti, cioe - ·
da li quali se principiano tutte
le
littere cancellare=
sche,
Deli quali dui tratti l'uno é piano et
grosso,

Italic (Chancery Cursive), 15th C. to 16th.

its origin in the Renaissance. When 15th century Italian scholars and artists required letters that were suitable for writing books, they aban-

doned the cramped, angular Black letters in
herited from professional scribes in the north
regions of Europe for a bookhand that flowed
across the page with the rhythm of an arcade.
Because of their concern with ancient literature
the humanists favored 9th century letterforms
from the writings of the Holy Roman Empire,
mistakenly thinking that they were authentic
examples of writing from ancient Rome. They
selected their cherished 'Roman' models with
reverence for historic authenticity but primarily
for ease of reading the letters in book format.
Italian manuscripts produced after the year 1400
also display rapidly written versions of the new
humanist letters with well-developed rhythmic
arcades and elliptical shapes—the classic characteristics of handwriting movement. When written rhythmically the 'ideal' forms of the humanist bookhand became an orderly system of
cursive handwriting as lively and personal as the
writer producing it.

The development of a graceful hand with
natural cursive characteristics like those of the
15th century humanist cursive would have been
unthinkable in the beginning centuries of ancient Roman culture. Our modern alphabet was
virtually complete by the 3rd century BC, serv-
ing both formal and informal needs. Because of
the soft materials (wax, clay, even soft bark)

used to make all kinds of writing, the assembled strokes of archaic Roman letters lacked a rhythmic appearance. The stylus, the pointed writing tool used to form the letters, had to plow through the soft surface, leaving disconnected strokes. Technical improvements changed the process of writing from one of assembling strokes to making rhythmic patterns. As writing became a smoother process with the adoption of reed, pen and ink for writing on papyrus or parchment, it resulted in a more dynamic product. Sometime during the 2nd century BC, a Roman scribe developed a chisel-edged version of the usually sharp-pointed reed used for ink work. This new tool introduced a thick/thin

AIOFMSVKE

Archaic Latin Capitals from 7th C. BC. Preceded by Graeco-Phoenician and Etruscan alphabets.

ABCDEM

Reed Written Capitals, 2nd C. BC to 6th C. AD.

pattern of writing strokes that contributed sub-
stantially to their visual rhythm. Referring to
the ancient broad-edged writing instrument, the
famous 20th century British calligrapher
Edward Johnston commented, 'The most nota-
ble and perhaps the most important virtue of the
formal pen is this, that it has been the historic
letter-making instrument, having practically
created the innumerable types of lower-case
from the stylus-made skeleton "scribbled" form

Late Roman Cursive, 4th C. AD to 8th.

Late Roman Cursive, 4th C. AD to 8th.

of the 1st to the 3rd century.' Pen angles and letter proportions changed drastically with the energy and momentum of rapid writing. As the release of the energy channeled into new movement patterns, stray strokes soared above the writing space or descended well below it to create formal and informal letter designs.

This evolution of writing coincided with major social reorganizations; just as spoken languages took on unique characteristics, in writing centers in various areas of Europe individual national scripts emerged from the collapsing Roman empire in the 5th century AD. A

a. ΛBCDEΜ

b. ΛBCDEFM

c. abcdeɼʒ

a. Uncial Capitals, 3rd–4th C. AD to 12th.
b. Rustic Capitals, 3rd–4th C. AD to 12th.
c. Half-uncial, 4th–5th C. AD to 9th C.

borrowed collection of Roman capitals, Rustics, Uncials and Half-uncials served as a foundation for the major styles of writing in the British Isles, Spain, France and Italy during the following few centuries. Each style except the Irish was more cursive than not, and each contributed some special quality to the 8th century letter model synthesized by scholars in the employ of

abcdefg

Carolingian Minuscule, 8th C. AD to 12th.

The 'mark' used by Charlemagne.

14

Charlemagne, emperor of the Holy Roman Empire until 814. With the help of scholars and scribes from many areas of his kingdom Charlemagne supported the creation of a uniform writing model to serve throughout his widespread bureaucracy. Carolingian discipline dominated the mainstream of European literacy well into the 12th century and later served as the focal point for Renaissance reforms.

For reasons that are not clear, 12th century Carolingian writing evolved into compressed and angular styles. The various styles of the so-called Black-letter were immediate family relatives with Roman, Uncial and the Carolingian but displayed features with thick, angular strokes that condensed and sometimes fused letter parts. The flat pen angle used for writing Black-letter resulted in dense, cramped stroke patterns with an unusual vertical thrust. The visual quality of Black-letter writing can be compared to the feel of a rough piece of cloth—thus the models have descriptive names such as Fraktur or Textura. In spite of the extraordinary design features, informal renditions of Blackletter developed alongside the formal models used for writing books and official documents. The cursive was an independent design and featured classic handwriting characteristics of free-flowing movement, letter slope, branching

Suaviter

Pointed Blackletter (Textura). 'Almost all strokes of lower case letters are broken.'★

Schwabacher fghijkl

Schwabacher. 'Both sides of *o*, *s*, *d*, *a*, *v* are rounded sharp points; characteristic *g* is crossed at right.'★

Sctē Mihael archangele

Fraktur. '*o*, *s*, *d*, *a*, *v* are half round and half broken.'★

bestimpte

Rotunda. 'Tops of *i*, *n*, *m* are broken; curves as in Carolingian Minuscule with tendency of breaking but without sharp points.'★

Lady Elizabeth

Secretary. A cursive form of Blackletter.

*Jan Tschichold, *A Treasury of Alphabets and Lettering*, New York: Reinhold, 1966.

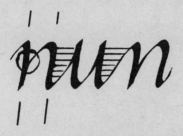

The essential elements of cursive handwriting: letter slope, branching strokes, compressed spacing and joining strokes.

strokes, compressed spacing and joining strokes.
Formal Black-letter designs grew through the same cycles of simplicity and complexity that other historical scripts had followed. As the novel patterns gained popular acceptance, elaborate, decorative variations followed. 15th century Italian Renaissance scholars who were interested in a formal bookhand eventually rejected this style of writing, terming it 'gothic' (barbaric). They demanded something more

readable. Their investigation of the earliest manuscripts available at the time led to the introduction of a modified Carolingian writing style in the professional writing of humanist scholars.

abcdefg

Humanist Bookhand, 15th–16th C. to date.

Quartus sculptor . Quintus

15th C. Roman type derived from Humanist writing.

Scholarly travels and communication distributed humanist handwriting designs throughout Europe. By adapting the Humanist Bookhand and its slanted variation, Italic, to print technology in the late 15th century, cultural reformers guaranteed popular use of the new models that became the hallmark of their renewal. The century-long growth of cursive humanist writing beginning in 1450 was the last significant development of handwriting in Western culture.

18

Later, masters of the 17th century initiated changes of style through new production techniques and writing instruments, exchanging the traditional writing instrument, the chisel-edged pen, for a pointed pen. Their purpose, during a period of shrinking demand for their service, was to sell their personal reputations as expert scribes by demonstrating dazzling virtuosity of

Saluator nostro diuinamente consolo,

Italian hand, 17th C. to 19th C.

a. *ABCDEF abbcddefo*

b. *Opportunity Oppor*

c. *Aa Bb Cc Dd*

a. English Roundhand, 18th C. to date.
b. American Business Hand, 19th C. to date.
c. Commercial Cursive Hand, 20th C.

writing skills. To demonstrate their prowess they simulated highly ornate results obtained by engravers who carved exaggerated Italic letter models into copperplates for printing books.

Pointed-pen styles dominated handwriting of the 1600s, and ordinary handwriting was confirmed as a 'fine art' preoccupied with elegant forms such as the British pointed-pen model called Roundhand. Commercial cursive models commonly taught in American elementary schools today are direct descendents of the ornate Roundhand. By the end of their elementary

Italic handwriting

CALM AFTER STORM

Through the night the sea thundered against the granite rocks and the west wind howled, rattling the doors and lashing the window-pane with gusts of hissing rain.

Italic Handwriting:
  Pointed writing instrument. (author)
  Traditional edged pen. (Alfred Fairbank)

grades, many students abandon their ornate commercial cursive writing, finding it to be too slow and accident prone for reliable results. Adults as well as students are seeking for a reliable alternative for modern, everyday writing. Because of its classic qualities and historic soundness, Italic is the solution offered by many educators and craftsmen. With successful traditions of tools, techniques and letter models, modern Italic provides formal clarity and informal freedom in due proportion in one and the same design—a perfect blend of practical strength and beautiful appearance.

CHAPTER TWO

Pens, Papers and Ink

BEAUTIFUL WRITING begins with a harmony of pen, paper and ink. After experimenting with many varieties of materials, most established craftsmen have personal favorites and regard their choices as essential for successful writing.

When a fountain pen works reliably it is no wonder that craftsmen treat it like a well-loved child, cleaning it faithfully and carrying it next to their heart. This sort of special pride and affection for a mere pen comes from understanding how important the right tool is for the job of writing. The pen becomes a sixth finger for the writer's hand. The point of the instrument must instantly respond to a continuous flow of thought with ink lines that glide over the surface of the paper. There must be a balance of strength and delicacy in the pen nib construction and a convenient, reliable inking system.

The pen is often taken for granted by the

average writer. In the case of the ballpoint pen, it is often a frustrating experience. This is something that everyone can identify with. A better alternative to the ballpoint is a well-made fountain pen. All fountain pens have some sort of ink reservoir in the barrel to supply ink to the nib, but the real difference is in the nib itself. There are many kinds to choose from, but one inexpensive style in particular is patterned in a traditional way with a chisel-shaped edge. The Platignum Lettering Set is one of several such

SPACING

One of the single most important facets of the art of calligraphy is rhythm, and rhythm will be achieved when you have uniformity of style, and also, regular spacing of letters. Thus:

unlimited

From *Lettering: An Introduction to Calligraphy* by Charles Pearce. This booklet accompanies the Platignum Lettering Set.

currently being marketed. It contains six graduated chisel-edged nibs, is reasonably priced, and it is sold with a thorough introductory booklet. A set of nibs for left-handed writers is also available. For beginning practice of letterforms in the next chapter the writer should use a large size nib.

The flat edge of this nib produces a shaded letter stroke that flows from thick to thin with infinite gradations when the nib edge is held at a

Writing with an edged pen held at a 45° pen angle produces the rhythmic thick/thin pattern of writing.

constant forty-five degree angle to the writing line. This rich visual pattern of Italic writing is not only unique in appearance but includes a practical benefit that safeguards the lettershapes. There is a definite increase of tool balance resulting from surface friction between the chisel-edged nib and the paper. This slows writing down to a more workable rate of speed.

A simple way to select the correct size of pen point for making a certain size of letter is to realize that traditional craftsmen always gauged the height of Italic letters in terms of pen-widths. For example, the body height of lower-case letters should be made at five times the width of the pen point used to write them while capitals should always be seven and one-half

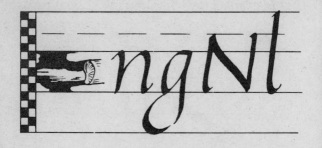

The body-height of Italic handwriting is measured in terms of pen widths—5 pen widths for lower case letters and 7.5 pen widths for capital letters.

pen-widths tall. Simply turn the chisel-edged pen nib so that its width is lined up alongside the writing page. Then mark the appropriate number of pen widths up from the writing line.

When considering the idea of fluent, graceful writing, the scribe must also think about holding the pen in a relaxed way. At all times grip the pen lightly. One author compared the fountain pen to a small bird. If it is held too tightly it will be crushed; but if it is held too lightly it will fly away. A good indicator of appropriate pressure in pen grip is the position of the forefinger gripping the pen. The finger should be gently curved rather than bowed with pressure. A cramped grip will shorten the writer's stamina for extended writing. If the pen is gripped correctly the non-writing end will be aimed approximately at the shoulder of the writing arm.

Use a relaxed grip for fluent strokes.

Unlike the fountain pen that contains its own ink supply, a dip pen must be recharged with ink by submerging the nib in a separate supply from time to time. Dipping the pen into the ink is a skill in itself. Do not plunge the tool in too far. Rather, stop when when about half of the pen point is immersed. The object is to capture a small drop of ink in the nib's reservoir. After dipping, wipe off excess ink from the nib on the edge of the ink bottle.

A droplet of ink is captured in the pen.

There are several fountain pen inks that serve well for everyday purposes. For example, Sheaffer's Skrip Permanent Jet Black gives adequate coverage. The slight 'see-through' quality of such ordinary fountain pen ink will help a beginning writer to catch errors of stroke sequence and direction. Unlike the india inks and so-called 'fountain pen india' inks, ordinary fountain pen ink will not clog a pen unless it is left uncleaned over a long period of time.

Any uncoated paper with a smooth surface will serve for beginning practice in formal writing. The typical approach is with 8½x11" white bond paper—the smooth kind that is uncoated and used as typing paper. Practice paper should be slightly transparent to allow the writer to see guidelines drawn on another sheet and placed under the writing paper. Avoid the papers designed as 'erasable.' Their writing surface is coated with a greasy substance that repels ink. For similar reasons avoid the use of papers designed for ditto machines.

After selecting the pen, paper and ink for the work, three other questions have to be answered before beginning the writing: What kind of writing desk should be used? What position should the writer use? How should the work be positioned on the writing board?

As a general rule, work on an elevated board. 'A flat table causes the writer to stoop, the manuscript is seen foreshortened, and the ink flows out of the pen too rapidly.' (Edward Johnston, *Writing & Illuminating & Lettering*, page 27.)

The elevated board doesn't have to be a fancy drafting table—a breadboard raised on two

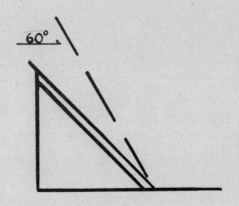

At first elevate the writing surface to 45° and later to 60°.

soup cans will do nicely.[1] The board should be angled at forty-five degrees up from the table. Eventually it should be raised to sixty degrees from the table, but this will seem inconvenient at first. Sit with the source of light coming over the left shoulder to illumine the work. The basic idea is to be able to see the work and to be comfortable.

Avoid extreme writing positions. Use common sense and work at a writing desk or table raised no higher than slightly above the waist of the body. Keep both feet on the floor and allow the body to turn naturally toward the work. Sit generally upright and relaxed rather than hover rigidly over the writing board.

To position the writing paper on the board, tape down a writing pad of two or three pieces of writing paper or a single heavy sheet to help cushion the pen strokes on the writing paper. Then position a lined guide sheet on top of the pad. Tape it into place, too. The guide sheet is simply a lined paper that will be seen through the writing paper and help the writer make the letters at the appropriate scale for the pen nib being used. The way to make a guide sheet will be illustrated a little later on in the section dealing with the letter models. On top of the stack made up of the pad-papers and the guide sheet, place the writing paper itself.

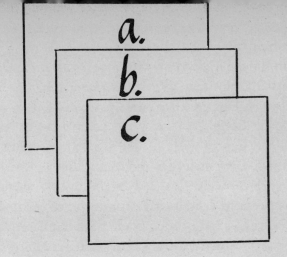

a. A few blank sheets used to cushion the writing.
b. The guide sheet.
c. The writing paper.

It is helpful to use a cover paper to protect the writing paper from ink stains and perspiration from the hands of the writer. Pin or tape the protective paper at the corners, allowing the writing paper to be slid freely upwards as the work progresses above the cover sheet. The entire set of papers should be straight up and down on the practice board.

To begin writing it is essential to have complete contact between the width of the pen point and the paper surface. Both halves of the split nib should be flush on the writing surface at all times. By gripping the tool lightly with complete nib contact on the paper, 'The writer should be able to feel what the nib is doing.' (Edward Johnston, *Writing & Illuminating & Lettering*, page 30.) See pages 34-35 for beginning exercises.

Move lightly with the pen at all times while writing. Be sensitive to the feel of the pen tip on the surface. Guide it slowly with slightly more pressure into downward strokes and release the pressure to a faint touch made with increased speed for upward movements. After reaching the bottom of a downward stroke, spring into the upward movement with control and feather-light pressure. The ink will flow from the pen at a slower rate and result in sharper edged strokes if the pen is only partially filled with ink. Even a fountain pen with its 'constant' ink flow, will need to be wiped off occasionally, and to do this keep a lint-free rag nearby.

Aim the nib at a constant angle to the writing line. The broad-edged pen will pattern thick and thin strokes in just the right way without the writer even thinking about then. The forty-five degree angle of the pen is a rule for forming all letters, but there are even a few exceptions to this process. Sometimes it is better to thin out a stroke, and the way to do it is by flattening the pen angle slightly by turning the nib in a clock-wise direction as it makes contact with the writing surface. (Use this technique for the final stroke of *k*, the crossbars of *f* and *t*, the second and third strokes of *x* and the entire stroke pattern of *z*. The bottom stroke of *B*, *D*, *L* and all branches of *E* and *F* should be slightly thinned by the same process.)

Revolve the pen tip in a clockwise direction from 45° to approximately 60°. Horizontal and right-diagonal strokes will be thinner than usual and vertical strokes and left-diagonal strokes will be thicker than usual.

[1]The Pentalic Corporation offers an inexpensive, easily assembled portable calligrapher's workdesk that is available through artists' supply shops.

Rapid Exercises For Writing Movement

∧∧∧ ″n +

mmmmm

minimum minute

uu uu uuu

union unusual unity

ooooooo

onion conglomerate

∧∧ ∧∧

vivid delivery ivy

llll ☰ lll ☰

illness promises

Alternate 'necklaces'
of stroke patterns
with letters using
the same motions:
m n mm m mh
mr m p mb
uu u uuy uu s
ooo o ooc oooe
ooa ood oog ooq
mv v m w mx
mz z mvk m
uu i uul uij m
uf m ut

Part Two

CHAPTER THREE

Letterform

Mastery of traditional Italic writing with a Fine or Medium nib will improve everyday handwriting, and the simplest way for beginning scribes to achieve this goal is, first of all, to study and write the letters in a large, formal style. Oversized, formal writing can be practiced with the Broad sized nib furnished in any of the fountain pen sets, and then different sizes of nibs can be interchanged into the pen barrel as needed for smaller writing. The Broad nib is most desirable for initial study because the details of oversized letterforms, as well as stroke sequence, number, and direction, are easier to see and evaluate for needed improvements.

After practicing at a slow rate with the larger letterforms, the novice writer will want to reduce the size of the writing and join some letters for more fluent everyday work. The 'new' patterns of writing movement provided in the Italic models give the veteran writer a fresh feel for an old skill. The use of a chisel-edged fountain pen stabilizes the natural elliptical patterns of simplified cursive writing so that even the larger formal letter models suggest rapid, fluent movement. When safe letter joins are used to increase writing speed, the strokes are both graceful and durable in everyday rapid writing.

The secret of studying letter models is to learn their pattern of movement. The models represent a visible trail of pen movement, pressure, touch/non-touch, and must be regarded as living gestures even if the hand of the writer has

The dynamic movements of Italic handwriting.

already moved on. This attitude rules out slavish copying and views the models as knitted together in a visual harmony. The unity is founded on agreement of proportion, slope and other shape characteristics. The letters are not diagrams for mechanical reconstruction but tracings of light movements to be felt by the learner.

Study the number, sequence and direction of letter strokes carefully as guides to getting the idea of movement for the letter as a whole. Also learn the letter proportions (width and height) by memory work and by actually measuring a few samples. Other things to learn about the letters: how they change stroke slightly when joining with other letters and how there are sometimes alternative letterforms to use in certain situations. Draw through the letters, talk about them, and then write them slowly and carefully. Try to develop a sense of touch even by writing the letters with your eyes closed. By taking the work slowly and by being open to correcting and adjusting slight errors, the skill of writing will grow soundly.

Joining letters together allows for faster writing but requires proportionately more care. The writing must be easily read. That means that joins that break letters apart or stretch them into odd shapes will not be useful for fast, patterned writing. In general, the correct forms to use in joining lower case letters are illustrated as part of each practice page for the study of letterforms.

A following section of study deals with word-forms and concentrates on the rationale and rules for joining letters.

The proportions of most lower case Italic letters are 2:3. That is to say, the letter body width is only 2/3 as wide as the height of the body. Ascender and descender strokes are not included in this measurement. The exceptions to

Italic letters are only 2/3 as wide as they are tall. *i*, *r* and *l* are narrower and *m*, *w* and *x* are slightly wider.

the proportion of 2:3 are *i*, *r*, and *l* which are narrower and *m*, *w* and *x* which are slightly wider. Most capitals are 4/5 as wide as they are tall. A few are narrower: *B*, *E*, *F*, *J*, *L*, *P*, *R* and *S*. The proportion of this group of letters is 1:2. The letters are 1/2 as wide as they are tall.

A note on the rate of writing before beginning the practice of letter models: Letterform goes through incredible changes as we write faster. Shortcuts in letterform for the convenience of the writer's hand simply distort the forms for no other reason than the muscular urge to write as fast as possible. Legibility becomes a secondary goal while it should always be the most important one. While movement is the very definition of handwriting, it must be systematic and controlled movement produced at a moderate rate of speed to make letters and words that are easily read.

THIS SECTION illustrates the individual letters, both lower case and capital as well as punctuation and numerals.

How to Learn

Get the idea: Carefully study the details of each letter: stroke number, sequence and direction; joins, alternative shapes; letter proportions.

Practice: Learn how to work with appropriate speed and pen pressure for writing various letter parts in large, formal writing and smaller, informal writing. Get the feel of what it is to make the forms correctly.

Adjust the results: Analyze poor handwriting as it degenerates into an illegible scrawl. Evaluate the undesirable writing from the separate aspects of letter slope, space, size and production of the shapes as well as the speed of writing. Learn how to heal the 'wounded hand' (illegible writing) by adjusting each of these aspects of the written word back to the model.

See Diagrams A, B, C on next pages.

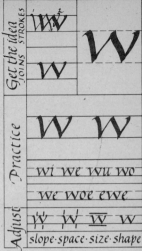

DIAGRAM A

1. Study the details of strokes, shape and joining.

2. Practice at a large, formal size and then try writing at a smaller scale for ordinary handwriting. Remember to use a guide sheet with spaces scaled at 5 times the width of the pen point used for the writing.

3. Pay close attention to the specifications of letter slope, space, size and shape. Use these diagrams to evaluate the work.

```
1

2

3

4

5

6

7
```

2 mm
B·3

DIAGRAM B

Cover the lined guide sheet with the writing paper so the guidelines show through. Never write on the guide sheet itself.

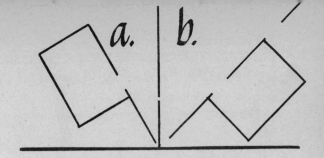

DIAGRAM C

Paper position for *informal*, rapid writing using:
a. Right hand for writing—tilt paper about 30° to the left from vertical zero.
b. Left hand for writing—tilt paper about 45° to the right from vertical zero.

For *formal* writing, position the papers in the manner described on pages 30–31.

Because the letterforms in the following pages are grouped wherever possible according to similarity of shapes and, in general, begin with the easier forms, learn and practice the letters in the order of their appearance.

Get the idea STROKES	*i̇ı̧*		*í*
Get the idea JOINS	*ini*		
Practice	*í* *í* *í* *í*		
	in ir iu ie io is		
	initial insight		
Adjust	*i* *i* *r* *i*		
	slope · space · size · shape		

48

Get the idea

STROKES

JOINS

Practice

ji jo ju je ja

enjoy job

Adjust

slope · space · size · shape

49

n

n

nun

Practice

n   *n*   *n*

ni no ne nu

nine nuns no

n n n̄ n

slope · space · size · shape

m m

m

m m

m m

mi mu me

mime mom

m m m m

slope · space · size · shape

hh

hih

h

h h h

hi hu ho h the hs

high how had

h h h h

slope · space · size · shape

52

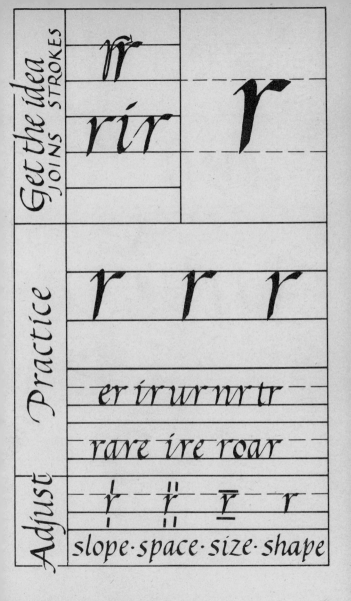

53

uu

u

unu

Practice

u u u

ui ue uo un ut

union cue up

u u u u

slope · space · size · shape

54

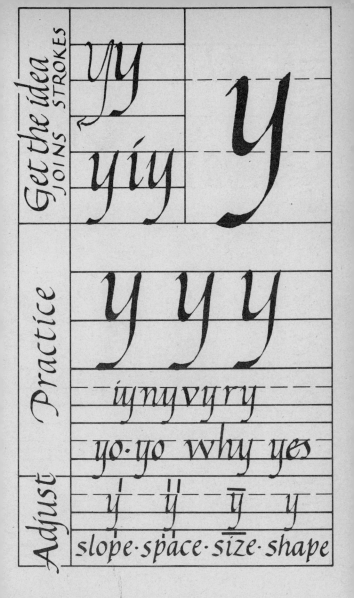

Get the idea
JOINS STROKES

yy

yiy

y

Practice

y y y

iynyvyry

yo·yo why yes

Adjust

ý ÿ ȳ y

slope·space·size·shape

55

Get the idea		
STROKES		
JOINS		

Practice

o o io

ac eo io uo

no no onion no

Adjust

slope · space · size · shape

56

Get the idea STROKES	*ẽe*	
JOINS	*nee*	*e*
Practice	*e*	*e* *e*
	ei eu ee eu eo	
	even need feel	
Adjust	*ʹe ʹʹe ē e*	
	slope·space·size·shape	

57

Get the idea
STROKES

JOINS

cic

Practice

C C C

ci cu co ce ci

cut cactus cot

Adjust

slope · space · size · shape

Get the idea	JOINS STROKES
Practice	
Adjust	

Get the idea — JOINS STROKES

S

sns

S

Practice

SSÍSÍS

sí su se so sn

suspense assess

Adjust

s s s̄ s

slope · space · size · shape

59

Get the idea JOINS STROKES	*a a*	*a*
	ai a	
Practice	*a* *a* *a*	
	anaiae	
	adamant again	
Adjust	*á* *ä* *ā* *a*	
	slope · space · size · shape	

60

Get the idea JOINS STROKES	d d
	did
Practice	d d d
	di do du de
	dandy dander
Adjust	d d d d
	slope · space · size · shape

61

Get the idea
STROKES
JOINS

Practice

ga gi ge
ragged tiger

Adjust

slope · space · size · shape

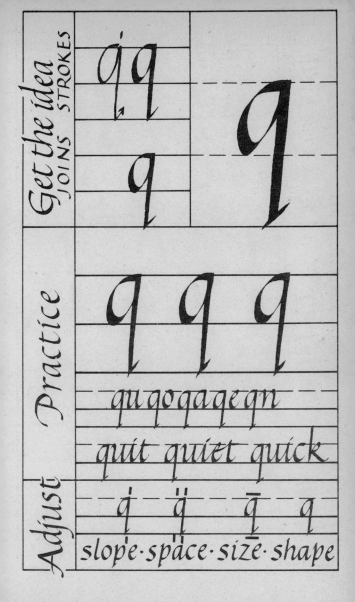

Get the idea
STROKES   JOINS

Practice

qu qo qa qe qn

quit quiet quick

Adjust

q q̈ q̄ q

slope · space · size · shape

63

Get the idea STROKES	ll	l
JOINS	lil	l
Practice	l	l	l
	ti lu te lo lr lt		
	hill hilt bell		
Adjust	i i i l		
slope · space · size · shape			

64

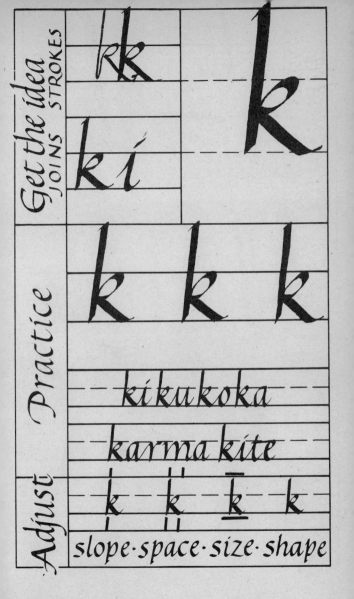

Get the idea
STROKES
JOINS

k k

k i

k

Practice

k k k

kikukoka

karma kite

Adjust

k k k̄ k

slope · space · size · shape

Get the idea JOINS STROKES	b b	b
	b	
Practice	b	b b
	babebib	
	bib babushka	
Adjust	b b b b	
	slope·space·size·shape	

Get the idea
STROKES
JOINS

pp

pip

p

Practice

p p p

ip ep ap up

pop pepper

Adjust

p p̈ p̄ p

slope · space · size · shape

Get the idea
STROKES
JOINS

Practice

Adjust

fi fe fo fu fr

friend fluff

slope · space · size · shape

STROKES

t

²t

t

JOINS

ntitt

Practice

t t t

ti tu to nt it

tutti frutti

Adjust

t t t t

slope · space · size · shape

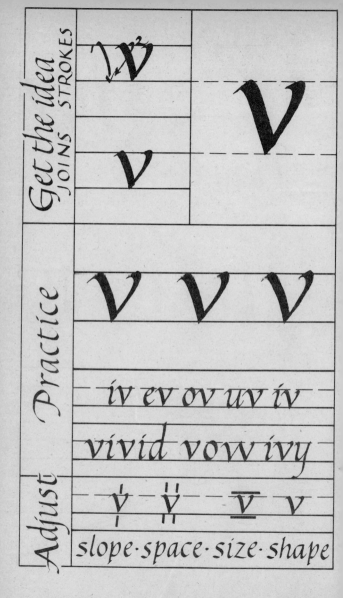

Get the idea JOINS STROKES	ᴡ	
		V
	v	
Practice	V V V	
	iv ev ov uv iv	
	vivid vow ivy	
Adjust	*v* *v* *v* *v*	
	slope·space·size·shape	

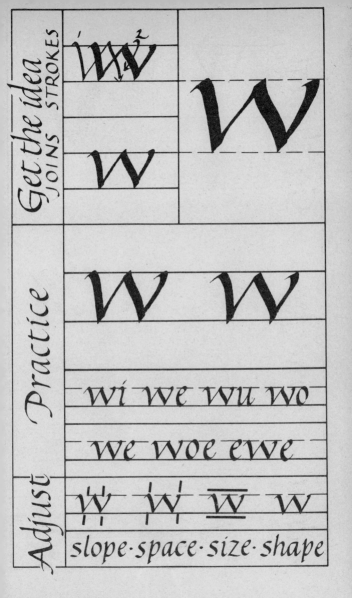

Get the idea
JOINS STROKES

Practice

wi we wu wo

we woe ewe

Adjust

slope · space · size · shape

71

Get the idea JOINS STROKES	Practice	Adjust

X¹ X³₂₁

X

X

X X X

xn xn

extra mix

x x x̄ x

slope · space · size · shape

72

Get the idea STROKES JOINS	Z z	Z
Practice	Z Z	
	ze zu zo	
	buzz zip zone	
Adjust	z z I z	
	slope · space · size · shape	

73

B L

E F

J S

P R

74

H A
N T
U V
X Z

Y K

W

M

O Q

76

D l

C G

E

(! ? ; : – ")

1 2
3 4 5
6 7 8
9 0

ABCDEFGH

IJKLMNOP

QRSTUVW

XYZ

79

CHAPTER FOUR

Wordforms

SAMPLES of correct joins are illustrated here and in the practice pages of the preceding chapter on letterform. The models illustrate a rationale for joining that serves the eye of the reader before the hand of the writer. The development of clear letterform for ease of reading is more important than speed in writing.

Rules for Safe Joining of Letters
Join into letters that begin on the right and join out of letters that exit on the left.

- Do not join into letters that have an ascender stroke (*b*, *d*, *f*, *h*, *k* and *l*).

- Do not join from the descender strokes of letters (*f*, *g*, *j*, *p*, *q* and *y*).

- Do not join with capitals or the following lower case letters: *b*, *g*, *q*, *v*, *w*, *x* and *z*.

a. *an b cn dn nen fn*

g hn nin njkn ln

b. *nmnn nonpq nrns*

ntn nun v wx nyz

a. The letter *n* is used to demonstrate correct joins into
and out of each letter of the alphabet. The letters left
standing alone are not safe candidates for joining.
b. Note the three kinds of joins: the roll (into the *m, n, r*),
the swing up into letters (e.g. into *i*) and the join made
with a crossbar.

Kinds of Joins

Joining into letters: roll over the top of the entry
stroke: *m, n* and *r*. Swing up into the entry
stroke: *c, e, i, j, o, p, s, t, u* and *y*.

Joining from letters: crossbar: *f* and *t*. Roll out
of the exit stroke: *a, c, d, e, h, i, k, l, m, n* and *u*.

THIS SECOND section deals with the composing of individual letters into words, involving the skills of joining and spacing.

How to Learn:
Get the idea: Study and memorize the simple rules for safe joins.

Practice: Emphasize rhythmic movement and an easy swing of writing gestures. Increase speed. Practice more often with the smaller sized nib to develop and use the practical joining skills in everyday writing. Besides copying the exercises, use a small nib in personal letters or notes.

Adjust the results: Check carefully for use of incorrect, 'unsafe' joins. The spacing of letters should be generally compressed.

See the lists of words on pages 84-86 for joining models.

in in union non
hunt dinner at
minute move
motion trees air
moment nation
number kitten
language prance

student cure
contributions
inspiration shy
astonish pledge
lumber forest
present joy it
give thanks

salmon trout
essay subject
responsible
ideal action art
center mind
beauty inward
fee·fi·fo·fum

CHAPTER FIVE

Pageform

THE CHALLENGE of creating beautiful spacing in handwriting is familiar even to a novice writer. From the beginning of their study of handwriting, students work with shaping letterforms according to right proportions and then blend them into groups for words. The formations of letterforms must be well aligned and have the appearance of even spacing. From these words the writer moves to the making of lines of writing.

To create pages of writing, the writer places and spaces lines of writing on the empty sheet of paper. Generous use of space around handwriting makes it easier to read. Traditional arrangements and patterns of line spacing follow on the needs of the reader for ease of reading.

Spacing Letters to Form Words
As the beginning writer tries joining letters for

more rapid writing, the spacing between the letters will automatically tighten because of the joins. Generally speaking, the writer wants compressed spacing because the eye of the reader absorbs clusters of letters in the act of reading.

a. *b.* *c.*

a. Space straight stems close together.
b. Space straight and curved stems closer together.
c. Space curved strokes closest of all.
The goal is the appearance of equal spacing.

It helps to have these clusters close together but not packed too tightly.

To create the appearance of even spacing, apply the following rules:

Space straight strokes *close* together.

A straight stroke and a curved stroke should be spaced *closer*.

Two curved strokes should be spaced *closest* of all.

Spacing Between Words
The space between words in a line of writing

should be a little more than the width of the
letter *n*.

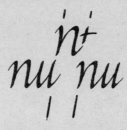

Space between words should be a little wider than the
width of an *n*.

Length of the Lines of Writing
For informal writing, limit each line to about 40
letters. If the lines of writing are too long, a
reader has trouble jumping from the end of one
line to the beginning of the other. If a line is too
short, the reader is bothered by the frequent
breaks from one line to the next. There is a
happy medium. For a simple rule, it is wise to
make each line of writing at least as long as 26
letters (one alphabet) and no longer than 52
letters (two alphabets). The average word is
about 5 letters long, which means that the average line of 7 or 8 words will be about 40 letters
long. The vocabulary of the author will deter-
mine the results.

_____ *26*

_____ *52*

For a general guideline, make each line of writing at least 26 letters long (equal to the length of one alphabet) and no more than 52 letters long (equal in length to two alphabets).

Space Between Lines of Writing
The writer should write in every third space to avoid interference of one line of writing with another. Ascenders and descenders have a way of interlinking if lines of writing are too close

Triple space between lines of writing to avoid mixing ascenders and descenders.

together. One solution is to shorten the length of ascenders and descenders, but the basic problem of line crowding is unsolved. The eye of the reader follows along the line of writing and must be protected from distractions that pull it to another line of writing.

Margins
Page margins are the spaces left around the edge of the body of writing on the page. They result from limiting the length of lines of writing so that the lines form a body of writing, a mass of lines. If carefully done, the lines will be limited

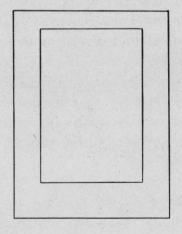

The rectangle formed by the body of writing should be proportionate to the shape of the page.

to a length that will make the body of writing into a rectangle that is proportionate to the page it rests on. Margins become a function of writing rather than an arbitrary control over line length.

There is a practical aspect of margins that serves the need of the reader for large amounts of white page space. Traditional layouts left about fifty percent of page space for margins. The tail margin is most generous of all. In the traditional layout it acts like a visual pillow for the body of writing. On a practical note, the reader is given adequate space to grip the book while reading. The head margin is narrowest, leading the eye of the reader directly into the line of writing as the page is turned. This minimizes the interference of turning pages while reading. In comparison with the head and tail margins, the side margins are an intermediate size and complete the framing of the body of writing. The single most important point in page layout is making the body of writing proportionate to the page.

Even and Ragged Margins

Line all writing lines on the left margin in an even pattern. The so-called 'flush' appearance is important on the left but not as important on the right. A ragged appearance of line endings on the right margin is common, but care should be taken to keep the lines close in length.

Always use an even, 'flush' line pattern on the left side of the writing space.

Single Sheet Layout for Handwriting
The standard paper size of 8½x11" is close to a simple ratio of 3:4. Allowing that design of the written pages is not an exact science, a solution for a classic layout (committing about fifty percent of page space to margins) consists in using a 1" head margin, 1½" side margins and a 2" tail margin. The result will be a rectangle in the center of the writing paper representing about fifty percent of the page space. Prelined student notebook paper presents an opportunity

Use generous, well-proportioned margins to set off the writing.

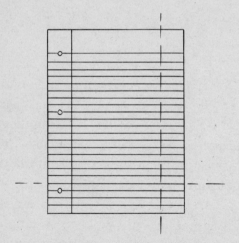

Take advantage of prelined student notebook paper margins to form a traditional page layout.

to accomplish the same task in a simpler way. Students could be taught to create a right hand margin on their notebook paper to match the established, preprinted left margin. They should begin writing on the first preprinted line at the top of the page and stop about two inches from the bottom of the sheet. The resulting layout is proportionate to the page and will improve the students' writing in neatness.

SUMMARY OF
NOTES ABOUT LEARNING PAGEFORM

THIS THIRD section presents a strategy for extending the skills of letterform and wordform one step further into whole pages of writing.

How to Learn
Get the idea: Study the idea of a non-arbitrary page layout for both formal and informal writing on vertical and horizontal pages using common, traditional page formulae. Memorize a simple rule for maximum and minimum line lengths and spacing between lines of writing.

Practice: Produce simple layout pages of both vertical and horizontal formats that demonstrate the page forms to be used with 8½x11" paper.

Adjust: Use tissue paper overlays to evaluate the layout theory used for various sizes of paper and various designs.

Part Three

PLATES

BIBLIOGRAPHY

List of Plates

Plates

Most resistance to the italic hand has come from people who had never tried it for themselves. But such of them as were in the end persuaded to make the trial were astonished by how much the edged pen remembers for you," producing thicks and thins with an easy certainty that wins and encourages the beginner. For here is a tool (long forgotten) that surpasses all expectation, & can be listed among the few co-operative' tools.

Paul Standard, N·Y· 1981

PLATE 1 Paul Standard

PLATE 2 Margot Thompson

Greetings –
Please continue
to enjoy the books.
Will come to dinner
after Easter. Am
commuting via
United to San Francisco
regularly now for
work in Bay area.

Prayers & best,
Paul

Catacomba di Callisto
Cubicolo dei Sacramenti – Rappre-
sentazione eucaristica – Principio del
sec. III

Stab. Pezzini - Milano

Charles Lehman
2828 S.W. Hume St.
Portland
Oregon

Reverend John Domin

Dear Chuck:

Its almost 4:30 pm. and we are still trying to make contact with Tom Gourdie in Portland. Phoned Jacqueline Svaren's home about 2 hours ago – her husband answered and said the Workshop would not be over until 3 pm.

Meanwhile, addressing these S·I·H·/B·C·B· Newsletters is making good use of the time as I sit waiting by the telephone

PLATE 4 Irene Alexander

JoAnne

Here are a few new members!
I promised them a quick reply
    and a weathergram book,
    hoping that's ok.
3 more days of teaching and I hop
    a bush kamikazi plane for the
    cannery and begin the annual
fish hunt.
Wishing you a beautiful summer
        &   Love
                Bill
June-26-1977

PLATE 5 Bill Gunderson

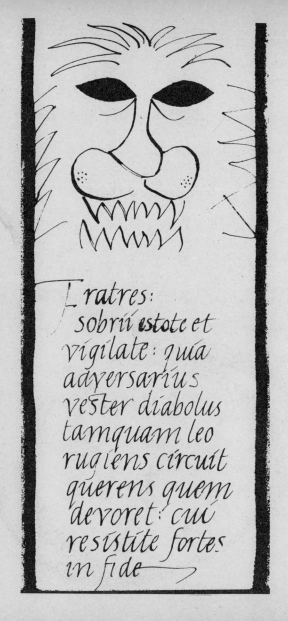

Fratres:
sobrii estote et
vigilate: quia
adversarius
vester diabolus
tamquam leo
rugiens circuit
querens quem
devoret: cui
resistite fortes
in fide

PLATE 6 Charles Lehman

Emmanuel, savior of Israel,
You are God's Son among us :
Come and save us, O Lord our God.
O Wisdom of the Most High God,
You rule with gentle might:
Come and teach us the way of prudence.

PLATE 7 Charles Lehman

Charles Lehman
c/o Tigard School District
Tigard
Oregon
97223

ABC

ASTORIA OR
DEC 7
1976
97103

PLATE 8 Bill Gunderson

say hello to all from me

It's been a long time since I've seen anyone —

Lloyd on weekends.

PEOPLE'S RIGHT TO PETITION FOR REDRESS

USA 10c

post card

Chuck Lehman
Tigard Schls.
13137 S.W. Pacific
Hwy.
Tigard, Oregon
97223

Königg House

This Harmonist frame residence (circa 1820 has been restored by Historic New Harmony Inc., and is now the rectory of St. Stephen's Episcopal Church.

Pub. by Historic New Harmony, Inc., Visitor Center, New Harmony, IN. 47631

dp DEXTER PRESS WEST NYACK, NEW YORK

Dear Chuck—Thanks for your letter & info. Very helpful! Will write to Eat—sounds encouraging—& to Mass. Waiting now to get reactions out— seem good so far. Will let you know as time goes along. Spring—hurry!!
Janet

PLATE 9 Janet Lorence

Yes, you're absolutely right. I expect to post that article later this week, along with proper apologies and a list of extenuating circumstances.

All the best. Briem

PLATE 10 Gunnlaugur S E Briem

Aesthetics
& History

Bernard Berenson

Anchor paperback

All sections on movement

McCarty
VICTORIA COLLEGE

University of Toronto

Toronto, Canada M5S 1K7

Department of Religious Studies

PLATE 11 Lloyd Reynolds/Willard McCarty

When i think of what
most men have to stick
their noses into every
day.... having the
opportunity to put mine
into a rose makes me cry!

Lloyd Johnson

PLATE 12 Charles Lehman

18 Bedford Row, London, W.C.1
24 February

Dear Pupil,

You have practised italic writing for some time and I hope you have liked doing so.

You will have learnt the rules & now is the time to check whether you are following them. Does your writing slant forward? If not, try to make it do so – but not too much! Do your thin lines run up like this //////? Are you finding some particular letter hard to do? If so, practise it. "Practice makes perfect", is an old saying. Is your writing even in size and easy to read?

Remember that your writing may give pleasure to your friends.

Yours sincerely
Calligrapher

PLATE 13 Alfred Fairbank

KENT COUNTY COUNCIL
KENT EDUCATION COMMITTEE

Staplehurst County Primary Junior School
Surrenden Rd. Staplehurst Tonbridge Kent TN12 0LZ
Headmaster K C Yates-Smith   Staplehurst 891765

Dear Chuck,

Thank you so much for your letter – without doubt
one of the nicest I have ever received.   Your very
kind remarks I have shown to all my colleagues and
read to the children: everyone has been most app-
reciative of your generous comments.

PLATE 14 Ken Yates-Smith

SELECTED BIBLIOGRAPHY FOR ART HISTORY

1. Arnheim, R.: Art & Visual Perception. Univ. Calif. Press.
2. Berdyaev, N.: The Beginning & the End. Harper. (P)
3. Berenson, B.: Aesthetics & History. Anchor. (P)
4. Binyon, L.: The Flight of the Dragon. Wisdom of the East.
5. Blakeley, R.: Meister Eckhart. Harper. (P)
6. Boas, F.: Primitive Art. Capitol
7. Buber, M.: Between Man and Man. Beacon. (P)
8.   "   I and Thou. Scribners. (P)
9. Campbell, J.: The Hero with a Thousand Faces. Meri‾
        dian Books. (P)
10. Carpenter, R.: The Aesthetic Basis of Greek Art.

PLATE 15 Lloyd Reynolds

11. Chiang Yee: Chinese Calligraphy. Methuen
12. Childe, G.: What Happened in History. Pelican. (P)
13. Clark, R.: Myth & Symbol in Ancient Egypt. Grove.
14. Clements, R.J.: Michelangelo's Theory of Art. N.Y.U.
15. Coomaraswamy, A.K.: Buddha & the Gospel of
16.   Buddhism. Asia Publishing House.
17.   "   Christian & Oriental Philosophy of Art. Dover. (P)
18.   "   The Dance of Shiva. Noonday Press. (P)
19.   "   Hinduism & Buddhism. Philosophical Library.
21.   "   The Transformation of Nature in Art. Dover. (P)
22. d'Alviella, the Count Goblet: the Migration of Symbols.
23. Dawson, C.: Religion & Culture. Meridian Books.
24. Dewey, J.: Art & Experience. Capricorn. (P)

Newsletter

The Annual Meeting of the Western American Branch/Society for Italic Handwriting will be at 8 p.m. Friday, March 26, in the Faculty Office Building at Reed College.

We are compiling a list of members who would like to correspond with others in and about Italic. If you would like to receive such a list & have your name and address included, please drop us a note right away.

PLATE 16 JoAnn DiSciullo

The Annual Calligraphy Exhibition by W.A.B. members will be shown in the Northview Gallery at Portland Community College in June. The show is open to all members of the Society. Start working now so that we can present a really good exhibit. If you would like to participate, fill in the following and send to the secretary. You will receive additional instructions and identification labels.

_____   _____   _____

Yes, I will show my work in the Annual Calligraphy Show :

name _____ phone _____

address _____

city _____ state _____ zip _____

Mr C Lehman

3519 S W California St.

Portland

OREGON 97249

United States of America

PLATE 17 Arthur Osley

Aug. 25. 1979

Dear Jo Anne,

After Manny's and your wonderful invitation, I am really ashamed to disappoint you as well as myself by saying that I am unable to travel this January after all. I do hope that I will have another chance to go west, not in a rush, stopping all teaching and other activities to really get to know the country a bit too. That would also give me more time to prepare 2 new subjects: History with slides plus workshop using the tools of each period and Hebrew.

I enjoy all your news by mail and tell every class of your society.

Sincerely, and regretfully yours,

Lili

PLATE 18 Lili Wronker

Frances M. Moore
320 East 72nd Street
New York
10021

24 January, 1976

Dear Chuck:

I was so ashamed, when I started to write you this letter,
of the long time it had been overdue, that I tried to get you
on the telephone — as you will undoubtedly discover when you
arrive at the school Monday.

Since I last wrote, a few more things that had to do with
my work have revealed themselves. I am enclosing them, along

PLATE 19 Frances Moore

INTRODUCTION

In J. W. Mackail's THE LIFE OF WILLIAM MORRIS, italic, c.&c.

he writes that for Morris and Burne-Jones, then

young Oxford students, Ruskin became for both

of them a hero and a prophet, and his position was

more than ever secured by THE STONES OF italic,
c.&c.

VENICE in 1853. The famous chapter "On

the Nature of Gothic," long afterwards lovingly

reprinted by Morris, as one of the earliest productions

of the Kelmscott Press, was a new gospel and a

fixed creed.

No #

sing. qure

sing. qure

PLATE 20 Lloyd Reynolds

Chuck Lehman. Tigard Public
Schools

Admin. Office; 13137 S.W.

Pacific Highway; Tigard

Oregon 97223 · USA

PLATE 21 Denys Taipale

Gouache – if you want to write with a color, you use gouache (or at least my do in London and Montana) Winsor-Newton makes a very good reliable gouache. Gouache is an opaque watercolor – thus, writing is an even color with no washouts. Watercolors have a transparent base; gouache has an opaque base. Comes in tubes. The best sepia red colors are "Scarlet Lake," "Spectrum Red," and Chinese Orange."

PLATE 22 Denys Taipale

TIGARD PUBLIC SCHOOLS

Learning
Center
Curriculum

GUIDE

&

DIRECTORY OF

Professional
Materials

PLATE 23 Charles Lehman

Italic Handwriting

These handwriting sheets are designed to help you achieve a fair Italic hand. At first you will have to write slowly and carefully but it is a cursive writing (not to be confused with lettering) and can be written rapidly and legibly. To this end we begin with writing patterns which help foster the cursive movement. The first page shows a variety of patterns which clearly illustrate the thick and thin lines, known as shading, which greatly

PLATE 24 Ken Yates-Smith

Dr. Lloyd J. Reynolds

18 June, 1902 — 4 October 1978

Prof. emeritus Lloyd Reynolds died of lung failure on Oct. 4, 1978.

Few people have been able to accomplish as much in their lives as did Lloyd Reynolds. His passing will be a source of deep sorrow to all who knew & loved him but his spirit will live on as long as there is a scribe to write, a philosopher to speak the words of wisdom, a teacher to brighten the lives of students, or a poet to give rhythmic flow to meaningful words. Lloyd was recognized throughout America and Europe as an eminent scribe & teacher. His fame as an educator attracted national attention while he was teaching at Reed College & even in his retirement years

PLATE 25 Robert Palladino

his influence continued through lectures and articles. A man of insight, gifted with eloquence and infectious enthusiasm Lloyd has led innumerable students to the love of art & literature as well as a deeper understanding of the meaning of life itself. The world knew Lloyd Reynolds as a man of letters but those close to him were aware that he was also a man of God. His spirit embraced believers of all creeds and helped them to love their own traditions. An outspoken critic of the materialism that pervades our society he spent his last bit of energy writing a treatise to expose and decry this evil.

Let us honor his memory by living the principles he taught by word & example.

Robert J. Palladino
5/oct./1978

Jonathan,

Remember to take the garbage out & to feed kitty.

Jim Cox called & wants to know if you'd like to go roller skating tonight in Mt. Vernon.

Stick around when you get here—dinner at 6:00. I have choir practice at 7:00.

Did you & Troy catch any fish? Clean them out by the garbage can, if you did & put them in the freezer.

Love,
Mom

PLATE 26 Janet Lorence

7423 S.E. 31 · Portland, Oregon 97202

Dear Charles:

Thank you for the note on the HARPERS' story. I did'nt know it was coming. Had the writer phoned an interview (or written) I would have told about you ⟷ your work.

Someone from THE NEW YORKER magazine is flying out to interview me in mid-June. Would you want to talk with him? I think that it might be good to arouse the curiosity of interested readers

PLATE 27 Lloyd Reynolds

Accede,
NUNTIA:
Dic, Ave, cominus;
Dic, plena gratia,
Dic, tecum Dominus;
Et dic ne timeas

Virgo suscipias Dei depositum,
in quo perficias Castum propositum
et votum teneas. Audit et
suscipit Puella nuntium; Credit
et concipit, Et parit filium, Sed
admirabilem. Consiliarium Humani
generis, Et Deum fortium, Et
patrem posteris, In pace stabilem:

PLATE 28 Charles Lehman

Go in person with a message:
    Say: Greetings!
    say: You are full of grace.
    say: The Lord is with you,
And say: don't be afraid.

O Virgin, may you embrace the gift
of God, and with His help, may you
 fulfill the Chaste promise, and, at the
same time, hold to your vow.

The young girl heard and embraced
 the message. She had faith and
 conceived, And she bore a Son
 (oh how admirable!)
The Counselor of the Human race,
And a strong God, the father
 of the people in enduring peace.

Thus the Light of light itself rose
 to us: thus a Man was born,
 formed of a Virgin, the Forgiver
 of sins who bore for us the fault
 of Sin and washed away the guilt,
 And gave us a heritage in the
 heavenly stronghold. Amen.

For small children, the mastering of various skills of handwriting is serious work and requires much practice. But too often their need for practice of skills is misunderstood by their teacher as a need for handwriting drills, that is, the churning out of a quantity of letter models — or worse yet, repetitious drawing of letter parts. This is certainly a form of mindless drudgery.

PLATE 29 Charles Lehman

Thoughtful practice centers on a clear idea of the goals of writing and then proceeds carefully with time for review of the results.

From the child we gather
the enigmas he left us, . . .
the songs he abused, . . .
his dark destination
which we now understand.
His word is revealed:
Behind every shadow

PLATE 30 Charles Lehman

grows the wheat,
An iris in each eye
without light. A rose
in its space of honor.
The hope which wafts
from the seeker. Love
brimming its cup. Duty

the pure bark of the wood.
Dew racing to greet
the leaf. Good with
more eyes than the stars.
Honor without medals
or castles.

PLATE 30 (continued)

PLATE 21 (facing)

Selected Bibliography

Anderson, Donald M. *The Art of Written Forms*. New York: Holt, Rinehart and Winston, Inc., 1969.

Cataldo, John W. *Words & Calligraphy for Children*. New York: Reinhold Book Corporation, 1969.

Catich, Reverend Edward. *The Origin of the Serif*. Davenport: Catfish Press, 1968.

Child, Heather. *Calligraphy Today*. New York, Pentalic, 1976.

Fairbank, Alfred. *The Story of Handwriting*. New York: Watson-Guptill Publications, 1970.

Fairbank, Alfred, Hooper, Winifred and Stone, Charlotte. *Beacon Writing*. Portland, Oregon: The Alcuin Press, 1979.

Fairbank, Alfred. *A Book of Scripts*. Baltimore: Penguin Books, 1968.

Farmer, Beva. *Italic Handwriting*. Carmel, California: All Saints' Day School, 1973.

Johnston, Edward. *Writing & Illuminating & Lettering*. New York: Pentalic, 1977.

Johnston, Edward, *Formal Penmanship*. New York: Pentalic, 1977.

Lehman, Charles. *Italic Handwriting* (Series). New York: Pentalic, 1972.

Lehman, Charles. *Handwriting Models for Schools*. Portland, Oregon: The Alcuin Press, 1976.

Lehman, Charles. *Introducing Italic Handwriting in Elementary Schools as a Basic Program for Handwriting Instruction: A Checklist*. Portland, Oregon: Western American Branch of the Society for Italic Handwriting, 1976.

Lindgren, Eric. *An ABC Book*. New York: Pentalic, 1976.

Nesbitt, Alexander. *The History and Technique of Lettering*. New York: Dover, 1957.

Ogg, Oscar. *The 26 Letters*. New York: Thomas Y. Crowell Co., 1971.

Reynolds, Lloyd. *Italic Calligraphy and Handwriting*. New York: Pentalic, 1969.

Reynolds, Lloyd. *Weathergrams*. Portland, Oregon: Western American Branch of the Society for Italic Handwriting, 1972.

Three Classics of Italian Calligraphy. New York: Dover, 1953.

Tschichold, Jan. *Treasury of Alphabets and Lettering*. New York: Reinhold, 1966.

/